"If you are so busy 'networking' and 'swimming with the sharks' that you have no time to thank the Lord for your blessings, then this book is for you. Read it at the table with your family. It will grace your life in an amazing way!"

—**Harvey Mackay,** *New York Times* best-selling author of *Swimming with the Sharks* and *Pushing the Envelope*

"In Amazing Graces, Dr. Gilbert has raised the simple blessing to another level of religious experience. His words resonate with feeling and inspiration — thoughtful and beautifully crafted expressions of thanks for the many blessings bestowed upon us by our Creator."

—**William G. Clotworthy,** Author of *In the Footsteps of George Washington,* and *Saturday Night Live: Equal Opportunity Offender*; a longtime NBC TV executive and producer

"What a bounty of blessings Dick Gilbert has given us! The velocities of grace and the gentle sacrament of family worship have been brought together."

—**William A. Emerson, Jr.,** Author of *The Jesus Story* and former editor-in-chief of the *Saturday Evening Post*

"*The prayers in this collection will prove a blessing to those who want to speak their thanks to God and don't know how. Readers will surely warm to having these table graces at hand for the festive occasions in their lives. The thoughts here are excellent and free of the usual cant of the traditional prayers.*"

—**Ernie Campbell**, actively retired minister of the Riverside Church in New York City

"*Ever searched for just the right words to express your thankfulness to God in an honest way that isn't super pious or pretentious? Here is a book of sparkling blessings — gems of prayer to thank God for the spectacular ways He has of being God and for the sublime ways He loves us. Dick Gilbert's prayers are magnificent expressions from a person who loves God with his mind and whose gift with words flows from a heart filled with wonder over His amazing graces.*"

—**Lloyd John Ogilvie**, Chaplain of the U.S. Senate, author of *Quiet Moments with God*, formerly senior pastor of Hollywood Presbyterian Church

Amazing Graces
Blessings to Season Your Meals

Richard Reynolds Gilbert

FOREST OF PEACE
Publishing
Suppliers for the Spiritual Pilgrim
Leavenworth, KS 66048

Amazing Graces

copyright © 2001, by Richard Reynolds Gilbert

Library of Congress Cataloging-in-Publication Data

   Gilbert, Richard Reynolds, 1924-
     Amazing graces : blessings to season your meals / Richard Reynolds Gilbert.
      p. cm.
    ISBN 0-939516-54-3 (pbk.)
     1. Grace at meals—Christianity. I. Title.

   BV283.G7 G55 2001
   242'.8—dc21

                                  00-053540

published by
Forest of Peace Publishing, Inc.
PO Box 269
Leavenworth, KS 66048-0269 USA
1-800-659-3227
www.forestofpeace.com

printed by
Hall Commercial Printing
Topeka, KS 66608-0007

1st printing: January 2001

To

Juanita,

who led me down a garden path

Acknowledgments

Among those who encouraged this collection, I must thank Jo Clotworthy and the sorely missed Patsy Warner who kept me at it. A bonus was the chance to revisit and reflect on the prayers of the Senate Chaplain, Peter Marshall, his inspiring successor, Lloyd John Ogilvie, and the angelic poet of religion, Samuel Miller. Closer to home, I must mention the loving influence of my writing daughter, Virginia, and my editing daughter, Allison, who went the second critical mile.

I look to the day when "older" grandchildren, Maggie, Nicky and Jack, will sit at table with "newer" grandchildren, Jake, Jasmine, Alex and Logan, to season their own food with prayer. And finally, I thank my "centennial" mother, Mary Cooper Christian, for the gift of life.

Foreword

To sprinkle light from heaven upon earthly pleasures — good food and fresh talk — is the audacious aim of this slender volume. Two intended readers come to mind: At one end of things are friends from Beverly Hills to Broadway, working in the arts or show business and living with color and excitement, who need table graces with spice and savor, even a pinch of poetry. At the other end are readers prone to prayer but secretly yearning for blessings that are brief enough to save the soufflé and artful enough to whet the appetite. With gourmet tastes, they look Godward to say with e.e.cummings, "now the ears of my ears awake and now the eyes of my eyes are opened."

Both readers, so different in experience, share a full-flavored taste for "grace," the amazing word that fuses gracefulness in style with gratitude of heart for blessings unearned. Thus the title, "Amazing Graces." And the afterthought, "Blessings to Season Your Meals."

May these graces, brief and occasionally playful, say "bon appetite" to some and "thank heaven" to others.

One

Lord of all space and time,
    if we fly, it is with your wings,
    if we paint, it is with your colors,
    if we eat, it is with your bounty.

Open our hearts and minds
    to the blessings of this table;
    may we share this meal
    mindful of your abiding care.
Amen.

Two

Boundless Source of all life,
  who has sprinkled the night with stars
  and softened the morning plants with dew,
  as we partake of this food and drink,
  teach us to thank you for the abundant earth
  and praise you for all that sustains the body
  and sweetens the soul.

Amen.

Three

For festive board
   or simple fare,
   for fish and cake
   or savory broth,
   for the cup that cheers
   and the plate that beckons,
   for the spice and tang
   in food or talk —
   for all these gifts
   and the meal before us,
   we give you hearty thanks,
O God of all provision.
Amen.

Four

Remember in your wisdom, O Loving God,
    those who have loved us,
    and those who have taught us.

Remember in your providence,
    O Compassionate One,
    those who comfort the sick,
    and serve the poor.

Remember in your kingdom, O Caring One,
    those who touch the aging with gentle hands
    and face a troubled world with courage.

May the food and fellowship of this meal
    give us the energy to treat each other
    with ever-increasing kindness and care.

Amen.

Five

Purify our spirits, O Lord,
    and give thy angels charge of us.
Launch us heavenward,
    that we may feel,
    both night and day,
    at this and every meal we eat,
    the sunshine from thy face
    and the gentle touch of thy hand.
Amen.

Six

We invite you, our loving God,
  to walk through the secret rooms of our souls,
  leaving there the marks of your goodness.
Save us from cold hearts and cruel words
  even as you warm the cockles with daily bread.
Amen.

Seven

Mighty God, who loves with a mother's care,
    hear our prayer for those
    in need of
    good health and bright skies,
    in need of
    tender love and boundless care.
May we leave this table strengthened
    for every battle of righteousness
    and every peaceful quest.
Amen.

Marywood
UNIVERSITY
Campus Ministry

Eight

God of all creation,
    who makes the stars to spin
    within the wheels of whirling galaxies,
    and whose power is manifest in
    surging seas and rushing rivers,
    it is yet your gracious love for the smallest life
    that marks your presence within this mighty planet.
Grace our table, we pray,

    with the power of that love.

Amen.

Nine

Holy and ever present God,
   descend the stairways of our lives
   and fill our hearts with gratitude
   for a land of milk and honey,
   and a meal of bread and wine.

Amen.

Ten

For the table before us
    and the friends around it,
    for the bread upon it
    and the cheese about it,
    we lift our hearts above us
    to the caring God within us.

*A*men.

Eleven

For daily bread and with it butter,
    for meats and drinks enough at supper,
    for sweets and tarts from countless marts,
    for food of the spirit in restless hearts,
    O bless our board, most bounteous Lord.

Amen.

Twelve

Holy Source of all creatures great and small,
   bless this food before us,
   guide our words beyond us,
   deepen our pangs of hunger
   that we may lust for what is right
   and thirst after what is just.

Amen.

Thirteen

God of this circling globe,
    whose world is not for us alone,
    help us see the miracles beneath our feet:
        countless insects taking form,
        denizens of the sea in coral kingdoms,
        new worlds flowering in alien Edens.
On lands where green things grow,
    may dew and rain wash clean your air,
    may green things grow in earth so fair
    for us, the fellow travelers in your creation.
May the food of this table
    nourish our hearts and souls
    to your ever-expanding care.
Amen.

Fourteen

Lord God of all that is and was and is yet to be,
   we thank thee for the night that restores the body,
   and for the day that magnifies the soul.
Receive our steady thanks for wine and bread,
   for lively talk and goodly table.
Amen.

Fifteen

Holy Creator of earth so fair,
    still our hearts with
    noontide air and nightly calm.
Give us moments each day, we pray,
    as restful as a tranquil sea,
    as grateful as rain-soaked flowers.
May your grace gently descend
    upon our hands and hearts
    as we break this bread and share this meal.
Amen.

Sixteen

Boundless God,
    as far as the eyes can sweep,
    as broad as the mind can glean,
    as deep as the soul can reach,
    your spirit enlivens our table,
    your love emblazons our lives.

Bless our eyes and mind,
    our soul and spirit,
    to savor your presence
    in these gifts of food before us.

Amen.

Seventeen

Great and Holy God,
   to know the extent of your glory,
   may we see you steadily:
      in part—with thinking minds,
      in whole—with feeling hearts,
      in praise—with nourished bodies.
Full of thankfulness for this simple feast,
   we pray.
Amen.

Eighteen

God of Hosts,
  in the heady mix of our lives,
  let us find you fast beside us,
  as close to our mouths as the food we eat,
  as near to our lips as the words we speak.
Grace our souls and senses
  to recognize you at this table.
Amen.

Nineteen

God of paradise,
  we eat of the tree of knowledge
  and claim to be as gods.
Brought low, we hear you walking
  in the cool of the day,
  calling our names, naming our shame.
Forgive our foolish ways, O God,
  and keep us as close as Eden promises.
As grateful as the Prodigal Son,
  may we share this simple feast before us
  as a celebration of your mercy and love.
Amen.

Twenty

God of patience and forbearance,
    vainly we seek signs from heaven,
    to bless our lives, our bread, our wine.

What burning bush or pillar of fire
    can light the path of God?

Why seek such signs when all we need
    is the tender face of Jesus?

In him, our table finds its joy.

Amen.

Twenty-One

O Boundless God,
    when we speak to you,
    our accents are provincial.
When we speak of you,
    we weave your nature into
    a tapestry of our own making.
Hearken to our confusion, Gracious One,
    that we may know you at first hand.
Bend to us, that we may
    find in our meal's communion,
    an abiding presence, a guiding power.
Amen.

Twenty-Two

As we thank thee, Father,
  for this daily bread,
  we bow our heads in prayer:
Forgive us, O Lord,
    for we know the good
    and yet do evil.
We mirror the world
    and yearn for heaven.
We know the truth
    but live with lies.
Gather us, Father,
    like lambs gone astray
    and show us thy perfect way.
Amen.

Twenty-Three

As we refresh our bodies
  with these gifts of food and drink,
  may we hunger, O God,
  for meaning in our lives
  and kindness in our hearts.
Amen.

Twenty-Four

From the dust of the earth
 you made us, Divine One,
 part of your architecture
 with its great and glorious designs.
Now teach us to love a natural world
 that mirrors God who made it.
Grace our eyes and all our senses
 to see your hand
 in the fruit of the earth before us.
Amen.

Twenty-Five

O God of time and space,
    who alone knows the fate of our souls,
    as we sit down to this meal,
    teach us to tend all creation,
    to love animals great and small,
    to treasure nature in its paths,
    to help our fellows when they fall,
    and leave your business to you.

Amen.

Twenty-Six

What matters most, O God?
Is it not thy peace?
What matters least, O Man?
Is it not your pride?
Humble our hearts, O Lord,
    that we may know thy peace
    as we drink to thy glory
    and sup from thy generous hand.
Amen.

Twenty-Seven

From Himalaya's tallest ranges
    to level earth by sea,
    we are fragments of creation,
    the dust of your mighty hand.
As we take this food and drink,
    mold our clay to your purpose,
    that whatever life may bring,
    we may spend it at your feet, immortal God.
Amen.

Twenty-Eight

In memory, Gracious God,
  you open the gates of the past.
In hope, you lead us through portals to the future.
In faith, you grace our table.
Bless our eyes and hearts
  to find your fresh life amidst this meal
  and preserve your presence
  in our grateful living.
Amen.

Twenty-Nine

As the sun rises and sets,
  as the tides rise and fall,
  we eat and drink and go our ways
  with scant thought of you at all.
As we are nourished by this daily bread,
  lift our minds heavenward,
  that never a sun will darken
  and never a tide will flow
  without you at our side.
Amen.

Thirty

In the morning of our lives
    when all is fresh and new,
    in the evening of our lives
    when we know not our end,
    pray search our hearts, O God,
    in this and every meal,
    that we may cease from fruitless desires,
    and find pleasure in common things:
      in loving bonds and fragrant foods,
      daily signs of your goodly care.
Amen.

Thirty-One

Let us give thanks for every good gift:
    for the musical ear,
    the dramatic tongue,
    the carefree spirit,
    the comic soul and painter's brush,
    for all who bring us song and dance,
    light and laughter,
    for the food and drink that grace our table
    and the hands that lovingly prepared it.
For these and every gift we are grateful.
Amen.

Thirty-Two

Gracious God, who loves with a mother's heart,
  whose subtle, unseen presence
  tends our sleeping and greets our rising,
  be in our dreams for a better world.
Be in our hearts that yearn to praise.
Be in our love that serves the needy.
Be in the hands that made this food
  and in the flesh of those who eat it.
Amen.

Thirty-Three

We thank you, Loving God,
    for food to savor and zest in eating,
    for love's perfume
    and childlike joy,
    for the radiance of life itself,
    your praises to sing.

Amen.

Thirty-Four

Merciful One, Sovereign of heaven,
   sweep clean from our lives the absorption in self.
Sound echoes of heaven into hearts that are true.
Bring back to our table the joy of fresh talk
   and season our spirits with gratitude.
Amen.

Thirty-Five

We bow our hearts,
O God of heaven and earth,
grateful for air that is morning fresh,
for branches heavy with fruit,
for breezes that blow at dawn,
for early light and evening dusk,
for pleasures of food and friends and drink.

Amen.

Thirty-Six

Lord of the table,
    as we eat and drink,
    gather and chatter,
    inscribe our talk
    with things that matter.
Amen.

Thirty-Seven

O Maker of endless skies,
    who once planted gardens about a fruitful earth,
    enlighten us, we pray, that we may know
    the wonder of common things,
    of herbs and grain,
    of aromas cooking,
    of special fragrances,
    of every delicacy born of grace
    and set before us with hands of love.

Amen.

Thirty-Eight

O God, there is no time or place
    in which you cannot be found
    if only we would look with the heart's eye.
Enlarge our senses that we may glimpse
    your love in the bread we break
    and in the glass we raise in grateful praise.
Amen.

Thirty-Nine

As we gather 'round this table, O God,
   fill our restless hearts with peace
   that we may be grateful
   for fields that bear fruit,
   for seas that set forth their bounty,
   for stars that steer a sailor's course,
   for all things rich in nature
   and all things wonderful in our souls.
Amen.

Forty

Lord God, the same yesterday, today and forever,
   yet ever-generous with thy surprises of grace,
   dip our sunless souls into thy light and color
   that we may eat and drink as children
   in the radiant presence of a heavenly Father.
Amen.

Forty-One

To fishers of the sea,
   to shepherds in the fields,
   to toilers on the farm,
   to all who feed your earthly flock
   and keep your people well,
   we offer grateful praise.

Amen.

Forty-Two

Sacred Source and Womb of Life,
    we turn aside
    from an unquiet world,
    seeking rest for our spirits,
    light for our thoughts,
    and nourishment for our bodies.
Give us thankful hearts
    and peace within.
Amen.

Forty-Three

O *God* of the turning season,
    we gather 'round this simple feast,
    giving thanks for common grass
    and running water,
    for snow and ice in winter blue,
    for golden fields and restless wind,
    for budding flower in early spring,
    for blessed sun on ripening vine,
    for tasty fruits in autumn time,
    for harvest in this world of thine.
Amen.

Forty-Four

Bless, O God, the daily tasks
   of home and hearth.
Bless with your maternal touch
   the hands of all who bring
   the wondrous yield of field and mart.
Bless the simple things—the holy things—
   that lift and lure the heart.
Bless this meal with your gracious presence
   each moment, right from the start.
Amen.

Forty-Five

O God, whose delight is the human mind,
 let us not turn your word into iron rules
 that build walls to the good and the true.
As we prepare to share this food and drink,
 let not our golden fancies
 harden into fixed ideas,
 but freshen our appetites for the feast of truth
 that thought may know no bounds.
Amen.

Forty-Six

God of home and hearth,
    may we be more loving of family,
    more faithful in friendships,
    more diligent in work,
    more patient with one and all,
    that coming together in your name
    we may be blessed as we sup.
Amen.

Forty-Seven

O God,
   from the charge of dawn
   to evening's peace,
   we praise you
   for morning melons and figs at night,
   for grapefruit and oranges,
   fresh lemons and limes,
   for ripe pears and cherries
   and sweet huckleberries,
   for pineapples, coconuts,
   nectarines too,
   the fruits of your giving,
   reminders of you.

Amen.

Forty-Eight

Giver of every good and perfect gift,
    be our table guest this day.
Adorn our words with color and mirth,
    pepper our minds with goodly thought,
    salt our ideas with common sense,
    cool us in shadows cast by grace.
Amen.

Forty-Nine

Gracious God, we pause to thank
    those we oft forget:
        the cook and waiter,
        the baker and soup maker,
        those who bring us fish and cakes,
        pastry and dumplings, jam and sweets.
In praising them, may we remember
    that the bread of heaven and the bread of earth
    are one from your generous hand.
Amen.

Fifty

O God of earthly tables,
　　we thank thee for our fare.
Be it the feast of celebration
　　or the luck of simple pot,
　　there is no occasion
　　that we owe not to thy provision.
Amen.

Fifty-One

How can we know you, Invisible God,
    if you escape our poor way with words?
Are you not many persons, yet one—
    Our mother so loving,
    Our sister so true,
    Our father so caring,
    Our brother so wise?
So, come to us, stoop to us,
    Spirit of the clan.
At this meal and at all times,
    tie our family into all that you are.
Amen.

Fifty-Two

With naught but wingless words
    and restless hearts,
    we seek thy "still small voice,"
    O God of silent mysteries.

Unclutter the doings of our lives
    and quiet the noisy clanking of our world
    that the very stars sing down unto us
    a medley of praise for this thy good provision.

Amen.

Marywood
UNIVERSITY
Campus Ministry